Michael,

Best wi

Success,

Roger

POINTS OF REFERENCE

(Roger Elkin)

POINTS OF REFERENCE

Roger Elkin

HEADLAND

First published in 1996
by
HEADLAND PUBLICATIONS
38 York Avenue, West Kirby,
Wirral, Merseyside L48 3JF

A full CIP record for this book is available
from the British Library

ISBN 0 903074 80 X

HEADLAND acknowledges the financial assistance
of *North West Arts Board*

Typesetting by
Roberta Morse, Priskilly Fawr, Hayscastle,
Haverfordwest, Pembrokeshire SA 62 5QF

Printed in Great Britain by
Cocker & Co, Berry Street, Liverpool L1

For my family and friends

ACKNOWLEDGEMENTS

Acknowledgements are due to the Editors of the various magazines and anthologies in which versions of some of these poems have appeared:

Acumen, Literary Olympians II (USA), *Orbis, Outposts, Oxfam Poems for Creative Aid, Poetry Nottingham, Very Green, Vision, York & District Writers' Circle Tenth Anniversary Competition Anthology*

The cover photograph is by the author (*War Memorial, the Island of Rab*)

CONTENTS

The poems in this collection though written in a variety of styles and structures have a common genesis in experiences gained abroad: Sections I and II from almost twenty years of visits to France; and Section III in a brief encounter on the islands of Krk and Rab in what might loosely be called the Istrian region of "the former Yugoslavia".

My original *Author's Note (1989)* to Section III read:

"*Visit To Istria* is not a travelogue, but a celebration of the stark grandeur of the Yugoslavian landscape as a backcloth to the dignity, tenacity, patience and resilience of a people which, though used to frequent violent invasion in its past, is now being compromised by incursions of tourists and the accompanying attrition of its culture and history in the face of western commercial values."

Sadly, politics have overtaken events, though, as yet, the Istrian region has not been dragged into the internecine bloodbath that has become Yugoslavia. Re-reading the sequence what is apparent is the continuing "truths" of the poems: as a celebration of former more harmonious times; and as a prophetic pointer to the pervasive historical and cultural tensions that have subsequently consumed the majority of the Balkan population.

SECTION I

POINTS OF REFERENCE

Beachcombing In Normandy

You will have seen how a marauding front of rooks
Will scavenge cross a field with slow, mechanical
Tread; stop; stab; then plunder savagely on,
So these beachcombers (women, kids and men,
Heads poised like birds, eyes cocked to the rocks)
Pick footholds at the turn of tide. Through a pool,
Then astride seaweed wigs drying in the sun

I follow them, and notice how the waves fall lacily
Upon the beach, the sand festooned like bunting
With kelp so artificially real it shouldn't be
Here. If it is not the shells — oyster scabs tinting
Towards rust, mussels stone-washed in denimed
Blues, and scallops's Spanish fans — magnetically
Dragging these folks to the far headland

Then what do they seek with buckets, bags and sacks,
And those with rods, and more with scoops and nets?
Gradually it dawns: it's crab, prawn, winkles, lug worm
That they want. (I'd overlooked the Frenchman eats
Almost anything except these sea-anemones, firm
Truncated stumps, tumescent in the bladderwracks.)
Ensnared, I too am pulled. Dogging in their tracks

And leaving sand behind, we soon achieve outcrops of stone
Where, conscious that they're aware of me, I stoop
To harvest anything of interest that my eyes light on.
Freed from the stratagem of their unspoken
Ritual, they suddenly stop and glare suspiciously up
At me: I have no prodding rod, or net, or scoop
So look back sheepishly, and half-propose a token

Clutch of shells. They stare, nonplussed, then scavenge on.
I wonder, do *they* wonder what I'm at, or have they thought
They equally are trapped? Would they begin to comprehend
Something there is that combs the foreshore of the mind
In which this scene, these sights, both catcher and the caught,
Counterpoint the onshore life my poem, rookish, thieves upon:
The plunderings left behind for memory's sport?

Omaha Beach

Seagulls cry alert: Mine. Mine.
Wave after wave assaults the shoreline.
Polished shells push explosively through sand.

Crabs founder like grounded tanks, or move
Amphibious and armoured, sideways and back.

There are carapaces and skulls, limbs and bones
Where they've gone over the top.

Starfish surrender arms for the cross of Lorraine.

Above, the sky is forget-me-not blue.

And, beneath feet, the surf is whispering
Vergissmeinnicht.

Game Market, Neuborg, Normandy

Faces like gargoyles from the church behind
French farmers are tied to history.
I claim true twentieth century anonymity.

Ghosting their futures, eight white turkeys
Shiver in a cage. The amber rabbits seem sad.
Quail, goose and dove have surrendered
Their pride to trade. Twelve lemon ducklings
Rhumba in a box. You'd be excused
For thinking their silence complicity though
Fear in their eyes reveals it's an asylum game.

Town wives haggle the price of hens packed
Two-deep in crates with all the crush, squeeze
And hunched alarm of Buchenwald.
Their sauntering husbands hold upended cockerels
Tied at feet, wings a-flurry like let-down brollies,
Later to hang headless in barns
Dripping their quilled skins dry.

I come for sights and photographs;
The French for food, or need, or is it greed?

It is straw they leave behind, and feathers
From dandy foul and guinea hens
More ordered in their symmetry
Than the rattlings of cash.

I leave, not entirely empty handed,
But trophy home this poem.

Feast handsomely on this.

Pavlova's Over For The Comtesse de Polignac

Now that the late Comte has been suitably mourned
in memory, she has turned his chateau grounds
into a camping-site. "After all," her butler insists,
"let's be practical. She needs to eat." He's
used to compromise, so doubles as receptionist
all summer and, off season, does the rounds
serving Côte du Rhone to cousins fixing eyes
on inheritance, or sisters anxious to be owned.

She's always known it wouldn't be long before
the society crowds and chairmen of the various Arts
dropped her from their lists. But is relieved to be clear
of Festival poets ogling over Pavlova and wine.
(Even her son, preferring Nice to Lyons, only reports
on Holy days and feasts, and always with another man.)

From April to October needs nothing from those
she knew, so has packed them away with her jewellery,
dancing shoes and gowns. Instead, keeps occupied
showing folks to camping lots, or trying to compose
notices, in several languages, that announce the
whereabouts of water. (She believes education
must be used to the full — then giggles at memories
of finishing-school in Berne, where Miss Eloise
introduced her to Sobranie cigarettes and gin.)

Of much that's fallen to neglect, she regrets the orchard
where fruit remain unpicked. And though sometimes sad
her husband spent much more time on vingt-et-un,
buying land and fillies, is rather pleased that he had good
taste in other things. (What would have become
of her had she eloped with that chap with Robert Mitchum
looks who stood her up in Grasse in nineteenfiftyone?)

In winter months, walks tall corridors and sepulchral
rooms, peeking beneath dust-sheets, or mentally reckoning
just how long the Gobelins, the still ormolu clocks will
keep appearances intact, and time unchecked, unbeckoning.

Ars Gratia Artis

for Ken

I recall your telling how last summer
Your family had strolled casually beside the Tarn
From Pont du Gard (is it upstream or down? —
I'm out of depths with geographical terms)
And pushing through gorged undergrowth, or
Sauntering along broad banks, noting the forms
That water had imposed on stone, you remarked how
Though folk got fewer there were more who
Had stripped all clothes and nakedly embraced
The sun. Somehow it seemed so natural yet raised
Some doubts about proprieties of skin. You questioned
Should you dare, but taking chance eventually found
Yourselves ducking in the river's chill, and with sleight
Of hand removed your swimming things, then feigning
Nonchalance waded, starkers, out. (The light
Sparking in your eyes conveyed a meaning
More articulate than words: the dare, the thrill, the fun.)

Now, this Christmas, comes a photograph-cum-
Card: the four of you standing in a line, not quite
Les Demoiselles d'Avignon, more the Bisto kids —
Two parents, naked as the time of birth, framed by lads
Coyly clad in trunks. Printed on your backs, four white
Letters in suntan cream spell out NOËL, somewhat
Incongruous against the sun and the river's blue.
While artistic licence covers matters such as these
(Like Life, most Art's a question of expedience) the compromise
Of compositional end and craft reveal that
You've considered, too, it's not so many folks who
Relieved to turn their backs eventually on work
Dare show their arse for sake of art. What cheek!

Away From Home

One thousand miles we drove to find a sky like this:
Bluer than our tent, big by day, and without cloud to all horizons;
And by night, bigger still, but black, sequinned with far stars,
Graced by moons.

In such open Paradise as this where space is ours,
The ground parched, but firm, beneath our feet,
And trees weary with dust, we celebrate our half-willed exile.

Lawrence would have envied us these lizards, pre-history's residual toys,
And from the picture-postcard-pool we can't send home
Hockney drawn a bigger splash.

Three weeks on, we find the openness confines.

By day, the mad-dog heat is overmuch;
We fear the mighty trousered bees deflowering tight petunias,
And since we've learned some will bite, we skirmish lizards.
Lost in its own reflection even the pool is paling;
Our talk half-baked as skins, we squat, soapstone buddhas
At its rim, squint against the sun and search each other's eyes
For memories of cloud.

Or by night, drawn moth-like round our lamp
Listening to the cicadas tzinging through the dark,
We yen for late summer rain in hedgerows,
The press of wet grass underfoot, the nettles' must.

It is times like these we begin to comprehend
The hurt in Bartok's haunted eyes, his music's pain.

August Dragonflies

Beauty has gone to more than your bulbous head,
Has infected your skin-thin wings
That ferry you terrorizing across the river
Where you're zipping yourselves to regeneration.

Your whole being is without modesty:
Not in aerobatics, or in colouring,
Or in your public promiscuity —
So practised and precise the thrust
So curled-coiled-spring the cantilevering.

Our children's stares and their kept breathing
Are no impediment to your breeding,
And we, explaining what you're at,
Surprise ourselves by not blushing.

Is it because
You only desire inheritance
That our words come as naturally
As your urgent coupling?

French Fireworks

I wouldn't say we walked — more like were pulled —
Through narrow streets close-parked with cars to Sete's
Port-side, where folks (excitable, well-oiled
With drink) were placed beneath the curve of night's

Vast cowl to watch the week's *feu d'artifice.*
Sharp crackers rocked the sky, while rockets spilled,
Stood air almost, then blossomed ochreous
And white like dead-man's-lace florets. Enthralled

By commentaries applauding man's success
In probing stars, crowds roared encores, aahed and
Clapped. This was no game: the seductiveness
Of Europe's "Ode To Joy" traduced to bland

Muzak revealed how commerce spawned with Art
Makes intellect a schmaltzy show, less sense
Of brotherhood, more sign of needing heart.
Your camera clicking at night's transience,

We stood and joked about relationships —
Remarked those sparking shows reminded us
Of making love: the jet of rising shapes,
Climaxing bursts, and falls to emptiness.

Next day, we searched for souvenirs — some squib
Or burnt-out stick. Nothing remained but dust
And ash. At noon we left the coastal scrub
And made inland; slow-zagged through mountains; crossed

The plain (cicadas tzinging in the heat);
Then flagged the final miles to Domme. That night
From crumbling battlements we looked on street
To homes located by their pulsing lights

Of galaxies more close than rocket-probe;
Then noticed, near our feet, star-replicas
As glow-worms flashed their fire-displays of love
In artless need as burning-bright as ours.

Points Of Reference

My wife finds comforting the cicadas' homing-calls.
I choose the river's quieter sibilants as it pieces itself
Together, syllable by syllable, voicing its being
Out loud like a child reading: I talk therefore I am.

Those practised aspirants angling through dragging
Hands; those hard consonants gravelling gutturally
Round its tongue, pushing its plosive pluck and pulls,
Flattening, then opening its vowels till it finds
Its glottal stops, slapping its wet voice against me,
Calling me to walk with its day-whine, its sun-song.

Its syntax pulls others: damsel and dragon-flies,
Rainbowed trout, kingfisher, roach. They too have
Their sentences in its autobiography.
Do I have a part? Or am I incidental
Like its name on my map, in blue,
Squiggly-insignificant and indexed for easy reference?

Sometimes I envy my wife's greater sense:
Her truths kept open like the cicadas' tzinging in the trees,
Her thoughts, like them, buttoning up as you draw close,
Sharing themselves between themselves and darkness.

SECTION II

FRENCH FRIENDSHIP SONNETS

Reaching Out

Docks left behind, we reclaim seats. A taut
Excitement thrills the ship. Those who haven't
Ranged to France before scan maps, re-plan routes,
Read kilometres as miles, re-invent
Itineraries, and rehearse their French
Crammed at evening-class or dredged from school-
Kid days. Recalling how once we launched
Just as ill-equipped, we manage our smiles,
Give tips but not the sum of years (after
All, experience cannot be taught) then
Sneak to duty-frees. We drink/talk/laugh to
Keep perspectives clear and sense since we've been
Invading France our lives have changed. Our ends?
Not getting there, but reaching out to friends.

Normandy Landing Beach

Humping windshields, towels and straw beachmat
On which to sprawl, we trog downhill. Just when
We question whether we've gone right, the path
Accommodates a turn then opens out
Revealing for as far as eyes can scan
Dunes, miles of sand, boats, and waves tipped with froth.

Seems calm, yet, underneath, the enmities
Erupt: shells explode through sand ... a star fish
Ransoms arms for life ... sea-anemones
Grow to bullet wounds ... and khaki crabs push
Edgeways, back, then flounder like runaground
Amphibious craft ... The images spawn
New landing beach where combatants become
These outpost words; the battleground our minds.

Questions Of Perspectives

Sunflowers to all horizons: huge blooms
The size of plates, they push to view their one-
Eyed lollipop-shapes fringed in amber flames.
What alarms is their massiness. (Lost in
Acres of these where could we turn? Their height
Rearing well above our sight, how much they'd
Terrorize.) Standing clear, though, plays of light
Emphasize how landscape makes their parades
Toythings of perspective. Later, in Tours,
Browned off by sun, we pursue cool streets. While
Remarking Renee Fonteneau's styles have
Used plant forms, we contemplate designs of
Need. Is friendship crafted so? Love, natural?
Or do they grow artlessly like flowers?

Going South

Almost five hundred miles we drove, the clouds
Nudged out by sun as we swept south where crops
Gave way to chalk, and tracks replaced wide roads.
Each bend we hoped the last, until we dropped
Late afternoon to valley's sudden green.
Exhausted by the heat we picked our plot,
Took time to pitch, then barbecued. That night,
Mellowed by vin de pays, we heard unseen
Insects tzing-tzinging from the clumps of fir —
Cicadas we presumed — and watched glow-worms,
Hyphens of light, pulsing through the dark their
Emerald messages of need. Such strange forms
Love takes. And lust? Then … "making friends" demands
Eloquent signs: from eyes, smiles, limbs and sounds.

Invitation To Attend

"Ambience assuré" the note declares
Boldly in red on white. The scrawled menu's
Inviting "potage; melon; pommes de terre
Garni avec herbes, et agneau en croute,
Petit pois; fromage; salade ou dessert";
And "beaucoup de vin" with each course. My wife,
Relishing food that she has not prepared,
Is keen; I hedge. What confirms the belief
She's right is when a huge Parisienne,
Immense in girth, small in height, leaves her cake,
Eases from her chair, and, with engaging
Nods, waddles to our tent. "C'est magnifique
Normallement, la fête." Her full mouths wets in
Ecstasy. "Fait accompli!" shrills my pun.

Dance Preparation

All day the campsite's fizzed: mesdames trotting
From tents to barns and back again, towers
Of cooking pots and salad bowls tottering
In their arms. Children, sent out for flowers,
Have returned with sheaves of vetch, marigolds,
Poppies, ox-eye daisies and greenery
Snatched from hedgerows. While husbands (once cajoled
From boules) set out benches, rows of laundry
Sinks have grown to lettuce swamps. Besides we
"Foreigners", the sole passive one has been
Our large Parisienne sweating in her
Chair. Now — the bunting fixed, trestles set, the
Wines dealt out, candles lit, musicians in
The bar — a stillness fills expectant air.

Disco Language

(Concores)

Inside, young folk are jigging at the bar;
Music's not bound by syntax, race or tongue.
The beat possessing them — strong, regular —
Means they've no need for speech. Instead they fling
All sense to gestures that declare intent
Of purpose: pleasure here, and now. What words
They share supply their wants: a drink, a taunt,
A dance. Friendship, perhaps, comes afterwards.

Outdoors, we parents — French and English — sit
And chance the learning time requires. Silence
Embarrassing, diction inadequate
(De not deux; par for pas) and wrong in tense
We're soon aware (and sooner than our kids?)
Amity's best expressed in deeds, not words.

Petanque

(St. Mamet)

We had not played this game before we met.
Instead, intrigued, had seen how patchy sands,
Loose gravels, dusts, or clays (baked hard by heat)
Lend consequence to those, who, shaking hands
In friendliness, adopt more serious
Attitudes than "game" suggests. Ritual
Maintained, the play begins. In curious
Pose (spines bent, and palms held horizontal
At line of eyes) they balance boules in hand
Until a backwards twist — and silver-quick,
Like lightning, flashes cross the playing-ground.
In our boules games we do not have their knack
No matter how we ape; but, falling short,
Earning friends, not points, is our end in sport.

French Blues (Cahors)

Juniper berries — firm, plush — we'd picked in
Earlier years from scrubland shrubs towering
Raungily above Cahors. (Their pilled skin —
Red-through-to-must — left scents like flowering
Yarrows on smeared hands.) This year, again, we
Expected secret hordes, but folks had been
There before us — our harvest cropped. Robbed, we
Picnicked instead. Drained dry by noonday sun,
Appetites dulled with heat, we sat, downcast,
Until a thrill of butterflies, French blues,
Littered the sky. They swirled, then fell to rest
In crests on all our outstretched fingertips:
No wonder, being picked, we must but choose
Extended hands to grace relationships.

Escargots (Beaune)

Just turned ten, our son condemns French folk, who
Armed with plastic bowls and pails, prowl through grounds
Made damp by showers and search for snails. So,
Each time it rains, he's demi-god, as, hands
Slimed by trails, he unseals from parted plants
Antlered slips of skin saddled with pearl shells
Nestling in his grip. To secretive haunts
Distanced from pickers' glance, he sneaks, then spills
Sticky blebs to fresh Eden undergrowth.
Not one of us condemns his Fall from grace
At restaurant meals, when he, Adam-mouthed,
Innocently requests escargots, since
Lads can't stay lads; besides which growing-up
Sets great store by hand-picked relationships.

Church and State (Digoin)

Moonlit night; dark under trees. About ten,
Old Renault van parks up: a priest and three
Nuns climb out. Sneaking away to wee, he
Smiles blandly, while we wrestle their tent. When
It's up, he's back. Nods. Retires. No "thanks". Nuns
Escape. Next day, cassock sleep-creased, priest gets
Up early. Wees. As nuns scratch food, he sits
Reading scriptures. We beam *bonjours.* They mince.

George, our French tenting-neighbour, is a Red:
Expounds against property and God, but
Offers fish picked fresh from Loire — pailsful — which
Reluctantly we take. Too soon, they're dead:
Gorgon-eyed. Feasting friendship's gift, we put
Etiquette to rights: thank George; damn the Church.

Aimez Vous (Najac)

Most days I'm drunk by lunch time. (Cheap red wine
And sun is my excuse.) Beneath poplars —
Diamond leaves falling though it's not even
August-end — I sit and sleep it off, or,
Maudlin, sing, "Nobody loves you when you're
Down and out." The French pair, next pitch, smile, then
Ease away. She angles my wife later;
"Like French … you … love?" she hints. Our turn to grin.
And, later still, while standing with our kids
Looking down Aveyron's swirling length where
Opaline green and turquoise dragon-flies,
Iridescent in the sun, use the reeds'
Rapier-tips as breeding-grounds, the monsieur
Explains, "Like peoples … drinks, sexes, sleeps, dies."

Déjeuner Sur L'Herbe (Najac)

Sun standing tall above heady rows of
Almond trees walling us from passers-by,
Rugs spreadeagled on stubbled field, what we've
Arranged is lunch. Not quite after Manet,
Heaven knows. Unlike his quartet, we drink,
Eat, and (you've guessed?) all four of us have stripped
To birthday suits. We didn't stop to think,
Came naturally — clothes off. Why be trapped
In Englishness? This is France. And our kids
Can handle nudity: neither sex or
Age has blemished their prepubescent deeds —
Don't turn a hair. While we parents shield our
Appendages, boy and girl full-frontal
Shrill in search of cicadas' mating-call.

Riding The Surf (Cap d'Agde)

Stormwinds far out to sea have made the waves
Angry. Instead of Enid Blyton calm,
Rollers crash, churning-up the past few days'
Aquamarine to brown. Though folks have come
Hording on the beach, few swim. In fact, it's
Just our three kids who (leaving their sunmats
Opened out like graves) have dragged air-beds, blown
Hard, to sea. Lying face down, each in turn
Navigates the swell, calculates the dip.
Just before the biggish wave, they tread place,
Angle craft jigging at the surfing tip,
Momentum held, till the sea's hurtling race
Explodes them, scared but laughing, on the shore:
Such *joie de vivre*, this comradeship of dare.

Anduze, Again

Hard it is even for seasoned traveller
Estimating driving-times that fine drawn
Lines on maps can take, or how strange terrain
Exactly looks. And tenting's similar:
No matter how refined the campsite guide,
Atmosphere can't be classed or starred. Symbols
Note facilities, not moods. What looks good
Detached by photos from the actual
Grows sad in heights of season, or when rain
Ensues, or the camera's truly-angled.
Our memories ransom us; so we've been
Recalled — to swimming-pool; sun; ice-spangled
Gins and tonics shared with friends; heat; and shade:
Empathy earned, not mapped or ready-starred.

Calais - Dover

Strange as it may appear, though as keen this
Year as last for sun, surfeit of it might
Lessen appetite; so (once the ferry's
Veered clear of docks; slipped past the harbourgate;
Inscribed slow curves where buoys locate a wreck;
And sailed beyond the pleasure-trips) we stand,
Kagouls to hand, up near the forward deck,
And search for home. Beneath dull clouds the land
Now looms to cliffs. (Doubtless you'd describe these
Towering walls marking England from *abroad*
A "nameless shade of white".) Truth slowly dawns:
Reaching home's not concerned with sun or place —
It's relationships. Friends (newfound or old)
Serve self; and harbouring them makes rich returns.

SECTION III

VISIT TO ISTRIA

for Philip Gross, and Sylvia and Geoffrey Kantaris

ancient infant words

Kurykta,
sound knife-edged, craggy as landscape
broken-backed on hard consonants,
mean and stark, but monumental
like karst stones, the white dust
beneath olive groves, the spade-deep soil
meted out between harebell and sun,
the earth dirt

Curicum,
sound more domestic, tamed:
the Frankopan campaniles,
the piled, polished stones in housewalls
and churches, the lean peasants eking
livings from nothings, the severity
of nets, the cuttings of cradles, of boats,
the rhythms of being, of death

Kurik,
sound hewn in blocks: chunk
leaning on chunk like stones the white
of curded goat milk, stones banked
in walls and the sons of walls riding
the hillsides, stones and shale of stones
in shallow graves of peasant and partisan

and the Batska stone,
ancient Glagolitic script
recording Croatian gift —
the sole atonement

Krk,
sound like the clearing of throats
spat out by a folk
that cannot rid itself
of the messages of stonedust,
the chiselled histories of stone

or bird sound that has swallowed
its vowels, its children
in the croaking of time

Kurykta   Curicum   Kurik   Krk

even the wind is divided

cruising the Kvarner Gulf
the sea is green and glass-hard
the horizon, between islands, a pure pale green light

to the east looking at the mainland
the islands between us and the mainland
are green as spring
with cedars, cypresses, olive terraces
and clumps of bushes lipping the shore-line
the clusters of pan-tiled villages
studding the coast

to the west looking to the leg of Italy
the islands are lion-coloured, dark bronze or bruise-hued
their bare hills shining like picked bone
where karsts have elided to sliding dust
and faces of rock look longtime quarried
(we wonder why the straggling walls
map the hillside crazily —
there is nothing on which even goats
can graze, the soil ochre and white and bare,
and everywhere stone   stone   stone ...)

in a land torn by history, nation set against nation,
Serb versus Croat, Mohammed against Christ,
even the wind is divided:
the bora a marauding middle-eastern force carrying
deserts to Europe,
the westerlies bringing rain in sacrificial spillings
blood on blood
Illyrian and Roman, Venetian and Frankopan, Uskok and Turk,
Hapsburg and Croat, Slovene and Kraut

whatever is taken, is wasted,
stone remains

we ate stone

Ate stone? Yes, time after time
till we had our fill of it

in olives, in plums succoured by dust
in apricots, hard and tasting of karst
in sunlight glancing from tall city walls
so bright it took our appetites away

had stone of mineral waters furring up taste
stone of dry white wines, the earth reds
stone in the glass, stone of local beers
stone in the must and bite of slivovitz

fed ourselves stone of the landscape, stone of the land
stone of stone walls going nowhere
stone of the sheep and goat droppings
and the bones of the gorged fish bloated on the shore
stone of the monuments, stone of the dying, the dead

had stone in the bora-gusts slicing the east coast
stone in the sea-breezes warming from the west
stone in salt-sprays lacing tanned limbs

tasted stone in squid, in lobster, in prawn, in crab claw,
the pebbled mussel and the name-unknown fish

ate stone in the oyster's liquid eyes

and (feasting our fill on the pedlar's jewellery
at his makeshift stall by the quayside wall
under the watchful gaze of the kommissar)
ate greedily the seed-pearls, the seed-pearls
stone by stone by stone

Ate stone? Too true, we did
                     … and worshipped stone

occasionally, that is

and worshipped stone

Sailing into Rab, one glimpse embraces the city:
at this distance a grey stone oblong, greyness
relieved by vermilion pan-tiles and four smaller
verticals — campaniles — that balance the skyline.

We disembark into full sunlight, penetrating
but unwounding, so no need for sunglasses
till late afternoon. It is almost a benediction,
this light, but menaces our eyes as we broach
the city's stone — not grey alone, but silver, or
golden rose at high noon, violet and blue
in the shadows, though always underpinned
by dazzlings of refracted whiteness.

Seeking shade and the sights, we climb through
tall streets, through coolness of stone, climb
to the cathedral's horizontal stripes of rose
and white marble like a sliced layer cake.

The door-grille is shut (it is noon, after all), but
jostled looks searching through glooms of half
light, scales of candles, shade and stone settle
on columns of cipolline marble, the tall baldacchino
over the raised altar with pyramided roof picked
out in tender red, and the vault above, a Veronese
blue. Nothing much else. Steps mounting to pulpit,
high carved stalls, unrelieved walls of stone.

Jaded, we retrace our way over the square, look
down between cedars to cobalt seas and secret
coves, but feel something, some force, dragging
our eyes back to the building. And there, raised
high over the doorway, a white pieta frieze in relief,
the Madonna sitting with stiff spine, chin held
high, sorrowful as sorrow, holding a Christ dead
as any skinned lamb for sale in the market place.
Dead as death. Just so much poundage of flesh.

The rest of our stay, we meet them, mother and
son, in the sculpted faces of the head-draped
women bartering in markets, the gossiping men,
fruit vendors, net-menders — that sacrament of stone
carried living before us, a dignity, a holiness
as weighty as worshipped stone, that simple
severity, guiltless as life, as stone, as prayer.

still vibrating blue

(Geoffrey's Poem)

By day, the still vibrating blue of the Adriatic:
cross between aquamarine and turquoise,
still as a leaning need out towards Venice,
but nearer — just beyond the swimmers
and the fishing trips — vibrating almost to graining
under the mid-day sun and the heat-haze
shimmering mid-distance.

At night, crossing to Malinska, still still,
but prussian blue or black almost, and like
some Covent Garden opera back-cloth, unreally real,
its crested waves luminescent beneath
moonlight as Drinkjak's water-taxi phut-phuts
through darkness. We sit up front, high on
moonshine slivovitz with its must of plum trees
vibrating under sudden July rains.

And still blue, but stiller, the harebells
veined with light we stumbled on beneath walls
in arbours of karst dust crumbling
under the sun's swollen heat and the moon's ghostings;
the fragility of need, an ever-so-slight vibrating
blue.
    What water, what sea is it that is pulled
through roots to menace so in delicacies of petals?

I am reminded of lovers' eyes. The sadness of loss.
The mid-summer lies.
The still
vibrating
blue

currency of memories

That day they brought the news
a confused stillness   an emptiness   a numbness
seeped through tall streets
slid across marbled pavements
(shiny and worn from centuries of feet)
scaled the narrow stepflights between houses
and strangled the afternoon laughter

That day folks huddled in dumbness
couldn't bring themselves to speak
(apart from the idiot-man who swore
his milk had turned sour
and those who pulled behind closed
shutters drank red wine
and planned reprisals)

That day even the sun seemed stunned
but the milking of goats
        spinning of silk
        mending of nets
just had to go on going on

That day the news was brought
that on the mainland beyond Belgrade
Danilo Pavlocic eldest son of the town
had been gunned down

                    *

Today in Tito Square a ten foot statue
rising from pools of scarlet cannas
laced with scattered dust
makes that partisan a national hero

Today the tourist books — Baedeker, Berlitz — do not mention it
do not mention him
and Carla our guide averts onlookers' eyes
with her broken English jokes then sidesteps
her gaggling crowd to arranged restaurants
and fat commissions

Today mother and father gone
his brothers do not talk of him
but at tavernas smile/joke/laugh
in monumental betrayals
as German lads chat up their daughters

Today senses drugged on the talk of inflation
no-one mentions the war
no-one reckons memories anymore

the dead have buried their dead

more delicate than mist

At that v just opposite the pizzeria
where the road forks along the quay
or uphill past the back entrance
of the Jadran Hotel, everyday, taking shade
from the oleanders, she sits, gnarled fingers
busy, faster than light. You don't see
the movement, not exactly each action
on each action, but a blur of hands,
a whiteness, and what she makes:
lace. And what she makes from lace.

An odd thing, this sewing together of holes
pulled out of air — an insubstantiality
that's antithesis to what she is: old,
dressed dustily in black, head scarved against
sun, face wrinkled and brown as walnuts,
arms wiry, veined, almost manly.
There is nothing delicate in her.

But from her fingers, and on the stall before
her, and draped on the lime-washed wall
behind, spin table-rounds, place-mats in squares/
oblongs/circles — there, there is femininity,
a newness, white against dark clothes and grey
shade, a hazy womanness that catches the sun's
whiteness and flashes it back in veils where her
ancestry and our today's greed are netted.

Hers is an ancient skill, threaded with the past,
piped, patterned, fretted, webbed, picked out
in broderies more delicate than mist, a fineness
that confounds today's brassiness, the tourists'
razzmatazz. It's a purpose in the haphazard craft
of life, a seeing things through to an end
resolved, circular, complete, made.

Rumour has it that in the last war
she laced her way in parachute silk.

inlaid pigskin purse

Since we're never at ease with bartering
we dead-eye the grouped embroidery girls
posturing at their makeshift stalls, and,
making fruit-sellers our escape, finger
plums, peaches, apricots, and taste the cheapest
grapes. Sharing pyramids of mulberried must
we saunter on, stop to gaze at rows of grinning
faces carved from wood (the peasants we have
seen have been refined by need, their faces
never so crudely caricatured as this schmaltzy
ruralism for the tourist trade). We drift to
leather goods — wide belts with brassy clasps
and stylised Indian braves — and compromise
the purchase of a wallet for an inlaid pigskin
purse, heart-shaped, palm-sized, so slim it
would slip inside a back-trouser pocket, nestle
neatly on a bum.

Back at the Jadran, inflation's rising — 5000
dinar to a German mark — drinks cheaper still.
We joke we'll soon need sacks for this paper change
replete with sculpted heads and heroic deeds.
To the bottom of our case we relegate the purse
(holiday gift/souvenir/totem of our greed?)
and sense its use will become less obscene
only with shifts in place and time.

more than bones — a holiday recipe

I   Preparation

Take one littoral strip, and discard
unwanted vegetable scrub (but leave
to one side the peaches and plums — some
run wild — along with the fish, prawns,
lobster grounds and mussel beds, not
forgetting the green olives: they'll be
needed for fillers later on).

Most importantly, lard the palms.

Following the contours of bone,
roll out the remains as flat as you can
but make allowances for a crusty surface.
Harden off restraining edges
but try to retain a natural form.
Dust it all down.

Dividing into moulds — flat after
flat after flat — fold rest into shapes of beds;
portion spare lots to squares (nothing falls
to waste) and squeeze leftovers into bars.

Lard palms again.

II   Cooking

Turn out early morning;
braise all day sunny-side up on a rising heat;
baste at intervals a.m. and p.m. with oil;
season with sea-salt according to taste; garnish
after eight with fresh coatings; dress up
goat/mutton as lamb, but don't allow to go cold.
Marinade in wine; shake, rattle and roll after
nine (or beat to consistency if preferred);
simmer on a low glow overnight.

III   To Serve

At all costs, cater for as many folks
as possible; keep always hot; best dished up
seven days a week from May to October
in full sun with oodles of pizza, ice cream,
coca cola and cheap local wines.

IV   For Dessert?

Push bones aside,
seek advice from the Kvarner Tourist Board,
keep larding palms:

you knead the dough.

cleaver in her smile

It is four a.m. and we have been
disturbed by the night-staff's singing
spree two floors beneath our room.

Voices raised, jokes and folk tunes ringing
through the dawn, they're high on slivovitz,
beer and fags. We bluster down

marbled corridors to the reception
desk where signs declare it's Magda's task
to meet requests. "What want?" she asks.

Focusing on her magenta lips, we explain
our need for sleep ... for calm ... for peace ...
the kids ... She nods. "Will see ow that's arise.

You right. No gutt for you, thees noise.
Will look". Her eyes are set; her pale face
fixed. Only her brilliant lips that crease

to something near a smile make any sense.
We finger the veneered desk. "Please,
it isn't morning yet, no more noise?"

"Will look. Gutt night." Dismissed, we
sneak back along the corridors, but stop
to note a female praying mantis (body

acid green) looking as if it's been propped
for ever here it's fixed so acrobatically in
the vast angle of the window pane.

Almost in slow motion, she articulates one
needle-thin limb, and leans out toward
her mate. He in turn slowly turns his head

dismissing us. We return to sleep. Next
day, half-past ten, we're strolling on the
quay and see Magda with the night-shift's

barman drinking beer. Her pale face pleats,
her lips push out a cleaver in her smile
that cuts our day-time peace to bits.

Twelve-thirty, back for lunch. As we file
through the corridor towards the bar,
we see the female praying mantis still

fixed there. Focusing on her magenta lips
our faces meeting with her butcher's stare,
we're once again dismissed.

Truth dawns: playing, we're preyed on here.

unlicensed trading

at the hour of stillness before dusk
when the tourists sink into afternoon stupor
(you know, that muddle of sun and sea,
that lazy haze of glowing limbs and mental torpor,
sun blushing above the horizon, and swallows
scissoring between trees)
that time before discos jig into business
and bars begin to get full —
at that time is the korzo hour when fishing villagers
gather at wells and street corners, and stand
in rumbled murmurings along quaysides

and, at the korzo hour, there comes, too, the crop
of traders — young men mostly — with thin square cases,
wooden frames, jewellery trays, shelled madonnas,
clockwork cats, pipe-cleaner birds in ugly colours
dancing to transistor radios in hubbubs
and on pavements where knots of tourists gather,
finger and pick, while villagers grimace silently

but the eyes of the traders are watchful, alert;
and — quick as nightfall — there are sudden
emptinesses with puzzled would-be buyers, fingers
handling vacancies of space, and only the thrummings
from fresh-started discos filling expectancies

at the korzo hour, the blue-clad kommissar
settles to newspapers, holsters his gun,
then lets them have half an hour more …

say his goats go well

he'll barter with Ivan for the boat
with an outboard motor
so he'll no longer have to depend
on his brother's goodwill;

or, say his goats go well, he'll
trade-in his battered van
that only goes with rocking
or parked always facing downhill;

or, say they go well, he'll
buy a new accordion, get an extra
pair of shoes, and stand another
round at the taverna where
no tourists ever go
(but keep enough cash back
to restock his flock)

but say they don't go well,
don't go, just don't go,
he'll call on his brother
cap in hand, try to hide his
scuffed plimsolls as he stands,
rock and push his knackered van,
master the sticking keys of his
dad's accordion, make his single
drink last twice as long

and come home for months
to goat ragout …

nothing in his net

Behind him the pebbled bay giving way
to the terraced village, hillside lilac with shade
and, higher still, pocked with outcrops of lime,
the on-shore fisherman, legs thin as dust,
picks his way across the beach, his net hanging
scalloped like a girl's gathered skirt as he stalks
water so clear his shins glimmer beneath.

Breath held, he checks; twists sharply as if stung;
then, swinging back round, arcs a single cast,
a kind of controlled violence, fast but yet slow,
that ripples through feet legs waist chest face
to be resolved in the stillness of uplifted arms.

The net, bunched bee-swarm-greyly at first,
sails opening out trapping sky in its mesh and
weights, hovers almost, then unfurls in gauzes
of haze, and shimmies into water, web sinking
though barely disturbing the surface sheen.

Hesitation. Then a forwards lean, a stooped
plunge from waist, legs kept straight, to drag
in the net, heavier, greyer now with its sagging
weight of water. Slow heaving, hand over hand,
pulling the round of the net's strands together.

But, this time, there is nothing in his net
save the rhythms of history, a ritual significance
that is picked up and cast down again, again, again
as he wades the shoreline, eyes torn between
the water's deeps and the power-boats scudding
towards horizons, the pleasure yachts.

Wrinkled like the back of his hands,
the sea makes everything its own:
reflections not worth harbouring.

naked to the waist

Sundays there isn't room to park:
the strip of sand that passes as a beach
is packed; pizzerias full, tavernas too,
the bars, the quay —

from Rijeka kafanas, the shops, the offices,
the reeking bars, the spit and little polish
of the People's Square they've poured across
the Tito Bridge — the Petars, Ivans, Vaks
and their wives and stringing kids.

You can sort them from the tourists
by their black-cum-navy bathing suits,
their gipsy looks, their lean and olive limbs
with skin nearing to unhealthy white.

And always their Yelenas, Katrinas, Annas
go just topless: pert breasts, nut-brown
nipples, unshaved underarms — go only naked
to the waist in a dignity born of poverty,
a decorum refined on need.

Further up the coast there's space
    (you'll know exactly where
      by focusing way out in the bay on the gang
      of adolescent lads sneaking a peak from their
      pedalos across striations of turquoise, azure,
      aquamarine as clear as deceit in the eyes
      of postcard vendors)
further up the coast if you go to that patch
of scrub where lizards startle with their wind-up
half-baked action, then through the auto-camping
with signs announcing "Our guests can make
use of the mature fruits of the fruit trees" you'll
come to where the oleanders proffering shade give
way naturally to the FKK esplanade and Hausfraus
lard themselves blubberish in the sun, all blistery-pink,
their tits heaving and wobbling, thighs shaking,
pubic triangles chiming — the whole full frontal
assault a mausoleum to the temples of plenty —

Going native for them doesn't finish at the waist …
dignity and decorum after all are only words …

Here it's marks, not Marx, that count.

46

full of customs

"Yugoslav eez people ov meny custom,"
the folk-leader explains to our upper
hotel-terrace packed with tourists granted
this once a week reprieve from imitation
Sting, Bros and Queen.
                          "Eez wan countree,
ov two alphabetics, tri religion, voor
speekings, five volk natives, sick republix
who touchings with sevan naybor stets"
(cynically we finish his mnemonic: ate
floor for theez otel, nines type local wine
testing sem, and ten? — ten plases
to eet feesh!)

Pleased with our game we giggle
intermittently through the first dance-set,
but ooh and aah at costume-wealths —
Slovenic drudles, Turkish pants, Grecian kilts —
as (stirring to fiddle, accordion and flute
in kolo after kolo, lesnoto on teskoto)
our feet and blood remember residues
of long times past

What steals our smiles is the Kicevo kolo,
silently danced, with the leading man
holding behind his back a clenched fist
in resistance against Turkish overlords

But what hurts more is the Yugoslav lads
in Bosch T-shirts and Wranglers turning
backs to overlook balconies and make silent
eyes at BMWs and Mercedes, turning backs
on lace and boat-building to look towards
customised bikes, don't give a shit
for goats and for fishing, turn blind eyes on
rituals of dance, on stones, lobsters, olives,
vines (even our student couriers training
to be advocates don't give a shit but
bleat goatishly "the air eez full ov customs" — have
unclenched fists for upturned palms ...

don't give a ... don't give ... don't ...